Lover Memories

Sony Dorai

BookLeaf
Publishing

India | USA | UK

Presentation by *BookLeaf Publishing*

Web: www.bookleafpub.com

E-mail: info@bookleafpub.com

ISBN: 9789363313958

First edition 2024

*To all the '90s kids struggling to find that
dream love of their lives.*

ACKNOWLEDGEMENT

Thanks to everyone on my publishing team.
This would not have been possible without the blessings of Maa and Baba.
Special thanks to my family, Silky, Anukul and all the individuals who inspired me to write these poems over a period of time.
Last but not the least, special thanks to Deepak Oga for all the motivation and patience for making this book go till the printing stage.

Love Always.

PREFACE

Most of the pieces in this book were written at different ages, locations and growth phases of my lifespan.

Some of it you will find super amateur, but all essentially embody the process of feelings and thoughts pouring out and wrapping around words to create a poem.

If the reader finds in these pages a sweet connection to a beautiful moment they must have lived, I will think my purpose of writing this is fulfilled.

Love Always.

My Lover

His twin dark chocolaty eyes
Are enough to captivate a girl's heart
But then also he uses his charm
To spellbound the one who is worth

His voice so soothing and comforting
Can make you forget your worries
He can make you believe
In fairy tales and all other magical stories

In his arm
you will feel so secure
Like an oyster safeguarding
The dew so pure

His gentle carefree touch
Can create waves of emotion
Making you lose yourself in him
Like a movie in slow-motion

It's hard to get out of his arm
Which is an expert level maze
How hard you try to pull away from him
But at last you lose to his magnetic gaze

His venomous kiss can kill
Your senses in a second
Leaving behind an urge to be
His prey till the world ends

Just after the kiss
His killer look can rip apart your soul
Making you stand in the
Middle of the journey with him as a goal

His tempting invitations
Are hard to resist
You have no other choice
Left but to assist

His thoughts rule your world
His cuddles make you smile
His smell makes you
Forget yourself for a while

And when you regain your senses
You find yourself drowned in love
Thinking about the whole episode
"Kyun, Kaise aur Kab?"

Kiss

I don't know how the weather was
I didn't even know how it would be
All I knew were those passionate eyes
Like a mirror in front of me

His glances were sharper than
The Prince's sword
His eyes became a substitute for mouth
Without any word

Nearer the sword came
Piercing my soul
Harder was it for me
To remain whole

I trembled, I fumbled
Tried hard to distract
But all my distractions
Did nothing to him but attract

I can feel his
Breath so warm
Inside the unbreakable
Chain of his arm

Eyes got closed involuntarily
To feel the divine
To empty the vessel of
Purest form of wine

His lips were trembling
So were mine
Heartbeats reached the rate of
Per minute ninety-nine

Mind stopped working
So did the senses
No passionate eyes
No more piercing glances

Only thing in between
Was the thin layer of air
Which was trying hard to
Push apart the pair

Despite the resistance
Four petals embraced each other
Like the waves of ocean
And the current of river

As the toxic and
Addictive touch was felt
Mind and soul
Started to melt

Nothing seems like before
After the deepest dive
Coz two living souls
Are now alive

So passionate yet so sweet
Was the unquenched thirst
Disclosing all by itself
"Yes it was the first"

Be Mine

I may be wrong
You may be right
I may have hurt you
U may have cried

But in the deepest core of my heart
You know I love you more than anything
You are my life, you are my soul
Without you there's no life, nothing

I promise to be your princess
with all the hugs and cuddles I gave
Lots of love and fight
is not what we all have

Be with me, Be mine
Bring back the light and shine
Come to me, my love
It's my sign of olive and dove.

The Fight

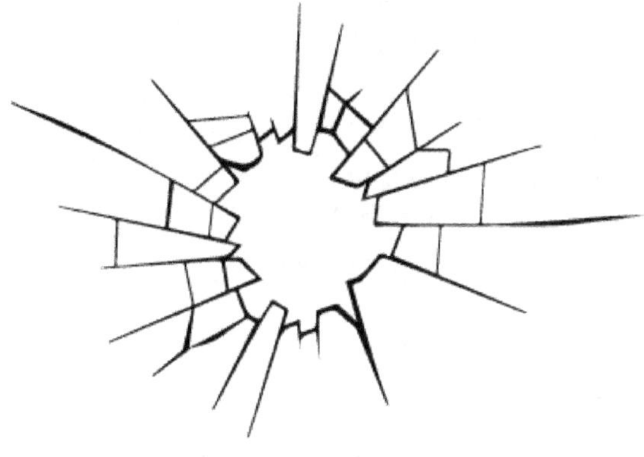

My greatest enemy of happiness
Never leaves me alone
Not in a crowd
Not even when everyone's gone

I hate how it snatches my smile
I hate it the most
My hands always praying
And hoping that it will get lost

But it always finds the way
Back to me
To make me miserable
And my life unbearable to see

I have changed the destinations
I have forgotten the paths
I have changed my present
I have changed my past

But it's true love for me
Finds me in the darkest place
I don't know where to hide
I don't even find any solace

It brings oceans of tears
As a "for granted" gift
And the burden of truth and guilt
That's hard to lift

Please don't come to me
I don't want to cry the whole night
I don't want to see
My happiness fading out of sight

When will "the fight" get over?
When will I be happy forever?
I fear it's some kind of nightmare
That will remain same forever.

Ajab sa Darr

Wo kehta Hai
"Use Phoolon Ki Chhahat Hai"
Magar jab phool khilte hain
woh unhe tod deta hai.

Wo kehta hai
"Use barish ka mausam acha lagta hai"
Magar jab barish hoti hai
woh kamre mein band ho jata hai.

Wo kehta hai
"Hawayein ishq hai us ka"
Hawayein lekin chale jab toh woh khidki band
rakhta hai.

Mujhe ab darr sa lagta hai
"Woh jab bhi ye kehta hai"
Ushe mujhse
Mohabbat hai.......

Apart

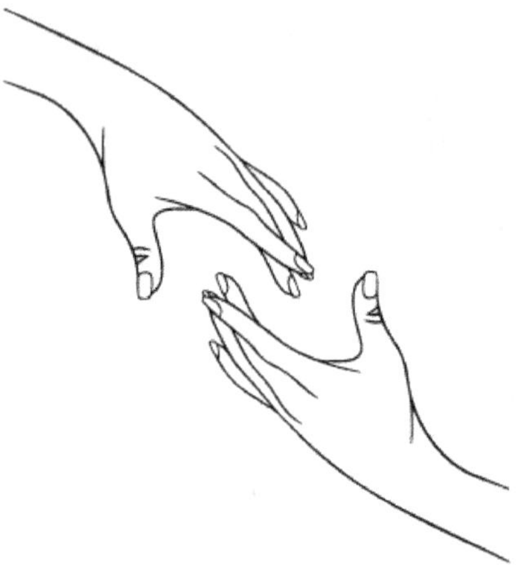

Her twinkling eyes reflecting
the reasons of her dimpled smile
Her charm and innocence
Can stop time for a while

His killer smile
With innocent, attractive eyes
Was the only thing for her
Beyond any price

Both were deeply in love
With each other
Like handful of dust
In a stormy weather

Silent promises were made
For the coming seven life
He will be the Man
She'd be the Wife

Lost in each other eyes
Like swimmers in a love-filled river
Him catching her every sight
Like a swift agile diver

Unaware of the high tides
In the full grown moon
They embraced each other
Like promising "We will be together soon"

But Alas !!
High tides engulfed their love
Thunder pierced their heart
Wind blew away their promises
Storms tore them apart

Only because….
High tides were her richness
Thunder was society's power
Wind and Storm were their
Own families' watchful tower

STD Call

*Tring tring….*oops
It's not the usual ring of telephone
It's "Baby I Like It" by Enrique
Ringing loudly on my smartphone

No matter whatsoever is in the
Mind of the other fellow
But the conversation always
Starts with a "Hello"

How was the day?
How was the food?
Your new friend-cum-boss
Is she good?

After all this formal crap
Comes the real bit
Like a hurricane before
The spring, ready to hit

One single word and
Years of bridging becomes useless
You start trusting your ego and
Believe in remaining hopeless

Then comes the routine
"I'm sorry for what I said"
Apology accepted as usual
With coldness of the dead

Some old memories
Some more jokes and fun
Life seems shining
Under the bright, big sun

Alas! The phone gets disconnected
Back to call log, I pressed "call"
But why on earth
A girl answered the phone
"Je nombor diye aapni call korche
Setha ekhon bondho aache
Doya kore kichu kon por dial koron"

After some time, again Enrique hits me with
"Baby I like you"
My old Nokia was out of charge
But now it's in full charge of you

Goodie, Goodie, cuddly, lovely stuff
With a goodnight kiss
And lots of virtual hugs and
An emotional "we will meet soon" wish.

Bored

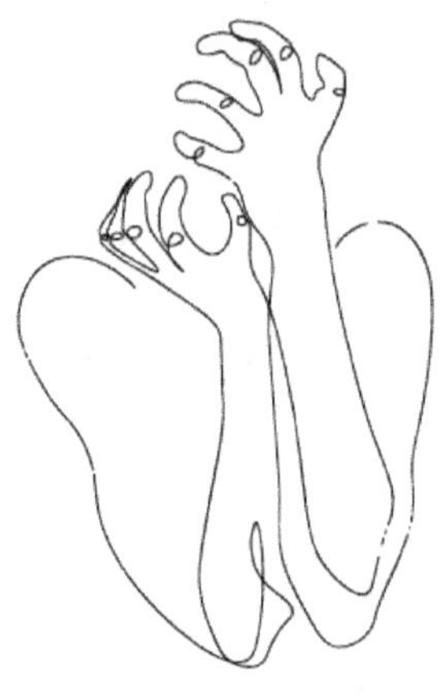

The new answer to "How are you?"
I'm bored
Nothing less, nothing more
I'm just bored
Life is running
At its usual pace
With my activities
Chasing in tortoise pace
How hard I try
To be alive
But it's all in vain
Like a rusted knife
I wake up everyday
With a dream
But it all gets

Melted as an ice cream
I want to prove myself
To the world
But the world views me like a
Picture so blurred
I don't know how to regain
My confidence
How to be awake and be
In my sense
Everything and every work
Seems so mundane
Working people make
me go insane
Take me out of this
Vicious circle
I'm spinning in these wheels of
An old bicycle
Yes!! I'm bored
Nothing less, nothing more
Just simply bored

Miss You

When the birds start chirping
When the sun starts shining
My phone starts ringing
For a sweet lovely "Good Morning"

But today there is—
No call, no "Good Morning"
I have already started missing something

The usual love and care
Past forgotten, secrets share
Always standing so close, so near
That's the way it was, my dear

But today there is—
No love, no care
No one so close and dear

The warmth of the blanket
The casual fight for internet
Lying on top of naked chest
With everlasting praise of curvy waist

But today there is
No one to praise, no one to fight
No one for me till the end of my sight

The swings on arm
The touch so warm
The "ugly duckling" charm

But today there is
No charm, no warm
No more ducklings in my barren farm

Much ab darr nahi lagta

Mujhe ab darr nahi lagta
kisi ke door jane se
Taluq toot jane se
kisi ke maan jane se
kisi ke rooth jane se

Mujhe ab darr nahi lagta
Kisi ko aazmane se
kisi ke aazmane se
kisi ko yaad rakhne se
kisi ko bhool jane se

Mujhe ab darr nahi lagta
Kisi ko chhod dene se
kisi ke chhod jane se
Na raat ke andheron se
Na din ke ujalon se

Mujhe ab darr nahi lagta
Akele muskurane se
akele aansu bahaane se
Na is saare zamane se
Na apne fasane se

Mujhe ab darr nahi lagta
Kisi ki narazgi se
Kisi ki pareshani se
Kisi ki bewafai se
Kisi dukh ki wafai se

Mujhe ab darr nahi lagta
Na to akele rehne se
Na to akele chalne se
Na apni zindagi se
Na ek din maut aane se

Mujhe Ab Darr Nahi Lagta...........

Dream

The moment I slip into my blanket
Sleep Queen comes around with her army
I try hard to fight against her
But get defeated by her mighty army

She never comes alone
With her comes her moody daughter "Dream"
She can be good, she can be bad
She can make you smile, she can make you
scream

She makes you believe that it's real
You try to run, you try to hide
You become the centre of the story
Played on the stage not much wide

You become invisible to yourself
Black and white is what you see
She makes your five minutes
Turn into an hour to flee

And as you reach the turning point
Her mother calls her up
Leaving behind no choice
But to get up

It's Over

I am done with you
You are no longer true
You lied to me
You hide from me

I don't say I was right
But neither were you
Now future doesn't seem bright
Anyhow with you

You show me your attitude
You fight without reason
Trying hard to pull us apart
In this lovely rainy season

After all the stupid fights
I tried to call you at 3 in the night
Just to get an automated answer:
"This number is busy right now"

I know you are seeing someone
Maybe she is the reason for our fights
Maybe she is the one you are searching
Maybe she is the one who is "right"

It's sad but true
We are done through
Yes it's over, my Lover.

First day

That morning, just after the rain
Sun was fighting to rule again
Wind was blowing in pain
Mother Earth was about to relive and regain

Yes, that was one of the wonderful days

I was loving the unpronounceable language
I was loving the crowd full of different ages

Bus was moving at its own pace
To help passengers complete their race

I was one of them
Distinctly different but somewhat the same

Just like others, I reached the destination
With baggage full of anxiety and emotions

The campus was full of inviting greenery
Reminding me of an artist's scenery

All in business formals
Trying to look different from normal

No known faces
Only "can-we-be-friends" type glances

I searched for a lone chair
To show I am also an alone pair

My eyes searching for someone "just like me"
But everyone seems to be a busy bee

But I loved everything about that day
Coz it was my first "Professional Day"

Lost

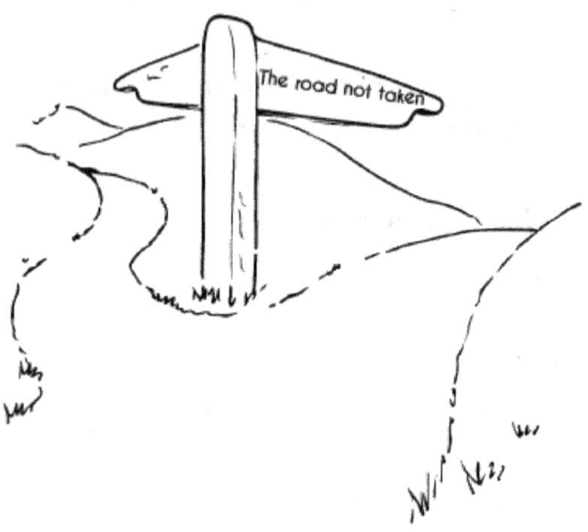

No one to comfort me
No one to love me
No one to support me
No one to hug me
I am Lost
Yes, I am Lost

No one to teach me
No one to hate me
No one to preach me
No one to wait for me
I am lost
Yes, I am Lost

No one to lose me
No one to betray me
No one close to me
No one to pray for me
I am Lost
Yes, I am Lost

No one to change me
No one to hide me
No one to exchange me
No one to avoid me
I am Lost
Yes, I am Lost

No one to scold me
No one to see me
No one to hold me
No one to be with me
I am Lost
Yes, I am Lost

Barbaadi

Barbaadi woh nahi jo tum dekhte ho mujhme
hum to abaad hai kisi ki bewafai se
itna gurur to khud husn-e-malika mein nahi hoga
jitna mujhe hai apne mehboob ki ruswai mein

In aansuon ko barbaadi ki nissani na samjhna
ye to bas ek zariya hai mehfil jamane ka
hansi ki to fitrat hai dhoka dena
par mere mehboob ko aadat hai ismein bhi
jeetne ka

Log na jane wafa ki kyun aas lagate hai
Jab bewafai me itni sachai hai
Wafa mein ek kharonch bhi barbaad kar sakta
hai
aur bewafai ki wafai hi mishaal hai

Humse jo puchoge barbaadi ka raaz
kasam khuda ki apni wafai ka naam lenge
Khud rehta hai mere andar yeh chalbaaz
aur ab kehta hai, "Chalo aise bhi jee lenge"

Loneliness

This feeling of being lonely
Kills me slowly

No one to hear
No one to cheer
Just me and my loneliness
In a heart full of emptiness

No matter how much
You cry aloud
No matter how much
You forgive and shout

This feeling never dies
This feeling never goes

This feeling of loneliness
In a heart full of emptiness

It gives me sleepless nights
With memories and me
In constant fights

This loneliness keeps on saying —
 "I won't leave you like him
I will always be there
Right beside you in all your cheers"

This feeling of loneliness
In a heart full of emptiness
This feeling never dies
This feeling never goes

Up above the sky

The day I was waiting for is near
No tension, no fear

I can now fly high and high
With my wings open wide
Feeling the blue sky
With no one by my side

Listening to the raindrops
Beside the rainbow shot
Getting closer to the cloud
To empty the rain pot

I can now see where the sun goes
I can steal stars
Make the moon jealous
And make her fight a war

It's so beautiful up
That I've decided to be here forever
With my new friends—angels
Always beside me here

Last Sip

I had enough of this enduring pain
With nothing to gain

I wanna end this up
Walk away, no looking up

I got my new identity
Having more of the mean equity

I love this way of life
"Living on the edge and being alive"

Never thought the smoke will be sweet
So much was there in a single treat

The dance in the "sheesha" bar
Was a level above par

The noise was so soothing to ear
Drifting apart the distance I fear

Rocked the floor like hell
Like a hurricane in a well

Enjoyed every moment with a sip
Dived into the crowd so deep

Forming cloud with smoke
Was all I remembered when I woke

My Day

Early in the morning
Get up and stop snoring
Kiss goodbye to your bed
Leave the tears that are shed

Start afresh like dew in a flower
Take a drizzled shower
Take your time to get ready
Coz you should look like a lady

Pick up the rosy brush
And make your cheeks blush
Get that mascara and kajal
Draw the lines with precision and angle

Don't forget the lipstick
That's the famous trick
Dress yourself in formal
Slip on the heels that are normal

Hang on, don't leave your Prada
Juggle the keys of your new Skoda
Drive her with attitude
No longitude, no latitude

Be the boss and rule
Try hard to be rude
Put things on stake
Avoid any mistakes

Don't be afraid
Leap some steps ahead
Get back to your Skoda
With your very own Prada

Entering "private life" now, wake up
Remove your makeup
Get back to your pajamas
Roll down some tears
For someone so dear

Don't feel so low
Just hug your pillow
Hold your blanket tight
And say a sweet good night

Toh kehte

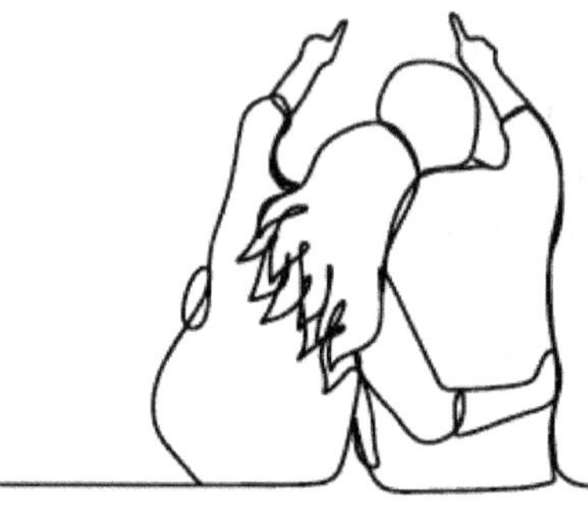

Hum duniya chhod kar na aate toh kehte
Waade saare tod kar na aate toh kehte
Kismat se lad kar na aate toh kehte
Rishton ki jaal se nikal na aate toh kehte

Hawaon ka rukh na mod dete toh kehte
Khusbhuon ko na samet lete toh kehte
Pakshiyon se na gawate toh kehte
Phoolon ki komalta na churate to kehte

Chanda ko na jalate toh kehte
Saamandar ko na tham lete toh kehte
Sitaron ko na chamkate toh kehte
Nadiyon sa na itraate toh kehte

Saanson se tumhari gulami na karwate toh kehte
Julf ki ghataon ko tum par na barsaate toh kehte

Naino par kajal na failate toh kehte
Hothon se jam na pilate, toh kehte

Bas ek baar keh kar toh dekhte!!!!!

Ring Day

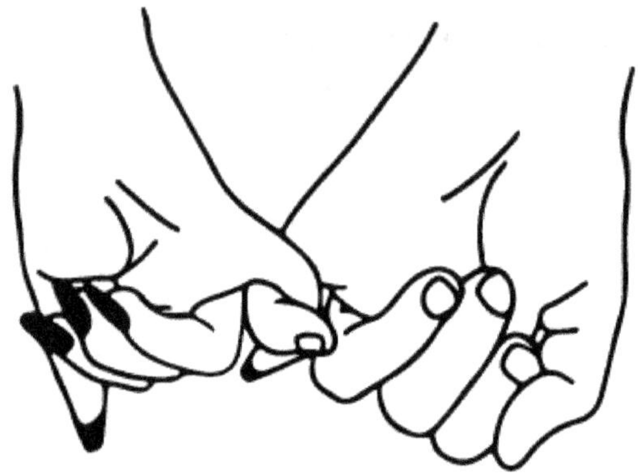

In the holiest of months
With the purest of hearts
You put a ring on my finger

No drama, no chaos
In the silence of my nap
You put a ring on my finger

No hint, no intimation
Just carrying the surprise in your heart
You put a ring on my finger

Size of the ring was not perfect
But the moment was as perfect as can be
You put a ring on my finger

That goosebumps from wearing it
Is etched permanently like the day
You put a ring on my finger

Dreams do come true
And finally, reality becomes better than the
dream
When you put a ring on my finger.

Seconds turned into minutes
Minutes into days
Days into weeks
And weeks into months
Finally, months reached a year

No wonder the twinkling pair of eyes
Will find its paradise
"And the flight got delayed"

Messages turned into calls
Calls into late-night calls
Late-night calls into wake-up calls
Wake-up calls gave in to video calls

Eyes couldn't get enough of his face
Ears kept longing for his voice
"And he was busy stealing the first kiss"

Winks turned into flying kisses
Flying kisses turned into stolen kisses
Stolen kisses turned into smooches
Smooches gave way to warm hugs

Shopping was just an excuse
Reason was to just hold her hand
"First date happened at Johnny Rockets"

Late-night dates continued
Hotels, restaurants, and casinos

Both complimented each other in red
She became his lucky charm Queen

Long drives to poolside talk
From Honda to Limo
From Nike to Rayban
"He slipped the ring on her finger"

Their love was unstoppable
Distance was just physical
Minds and hearts got entangled forever
"Couple" brought them even closer

From Shawarmas to Biryani
They learned to eat mutton and prawns
London Dairy gave them the chills
"And he made her drip Hershey's chocolate"

Not a single place was untouched
By their passionate love
Starting from car to flight
Bed to sofa, kitchen to bathroom

He was possessive about her
She was crazy about him
Both discovered their peace in "wanderlust"
"Finally, they made love in seven countries"

Their love was shining
Through the sky and the pristine ocean
Both love birds "gliding" high
Four oceans witnessed their love and sighed
"Their love has more depth than us"

The love was getting stronger
The time was passing faster
They bid goodbye with heavy hearts
"Istanbul cried when they hugged each other"

Priority

Call me
When I am the first and last caller of the day
Text me
When you really want to converse with me
Wish me
When you really mean it
Send me your picture
When it's been clicked solely for me
Travel with me
When you are not planning the same with others
Go adventure with me
When you quit begging others to join you
Like me
When I am at my worst
Love me
When you can stay true to me

Kiss me
When your lips won't touch another pair
Touch me
When you feel comfortable with me
Be with me
When you feel your world is empty without me

Else
You can mind your own business
I got a world to save

Baby

You are a liar and you know it, baby
I know you text her till you fall asleep, daily

You are a coward and you know it, baby
I know you call her every morning, accept it

You are a cheater and you know it, baby
You talk dirty to her and filth her, say it

You are a loser and you know it, baby
You give excuses that are baseless, forget it

You are a loser and you know it, baby
You won the game but you lost me, baby

Don't think I am a fool and crazy
I am ahead of you in this curve, let's face it.

Your Choice

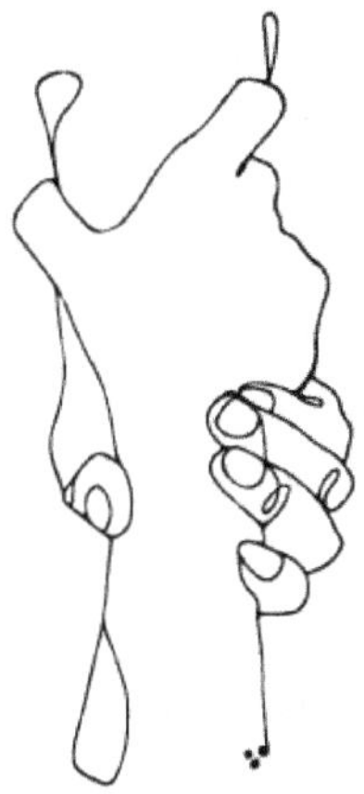

I was a normal girl
With normal Brown eyes
You fell for them in no time
And kept it in disguise

Finally the day came
When we met
Your eyes kept following mine
Whenever they met

"Friends with benefits" was not our thing
We knew we were more than this
Finally, the reality seems better
Than the dream I wish

Love was growing and
Spreading its arms
I felt so safe in
Your cuddle, so warm

But it didn't last long
We were sent apart
The last kiss was so
Hard on my part

You finally gave up
And said, "Let's break up"
I was devastated
Felt morbid to even wake up

But, my love,
Staying with me won't be easy
Leaving me will not be hard

Busy

Ping ping ping
My phone never stops vibrating
His messages always find time
To keep my phone ringing

From "Good Morning" till "Good Night"
He was never out of sight
From selfies to check-ins
He was always far ahead of stalking

His "online" was only for me
His status was quoted just for me
His last seen was after my text
My replies control when he'd come online next

My "Hello" was responded
With a minimum of six lines

His was the last message always
and never mine

His cute messages made me blush
He became a bundle of joy for me
His only work was to make me blush
My blushes were his prized possession

Till December came into our life
Cold, heartless December

No more blushes, no more pings
"Online"—what does that mean
Status for you was a past
"My life is rocking, and I am having a blast"

My last seen is for business, baby
Online only when work calls, maybe
Be happy with a good morning text
You don't know what I will stop next

Last seen are the cause of fights
Let me remove it and stay up all night
Selfies!! I don't click it any more
Ok, stop crying will send you one more

Happy??
Now he says he is busy
But never too busy for social media

Feeling Lost

Love came to me like the brightest weather
It was light and soft like a feather
I got drenched in it like a rooftop
Everything was under me, I was at the top

Full of giggles, full of surprises, full of pleasure
Moments spent together were like treasure
My world shrank, like a fish in a bowl
You were here, you were there, you were all
over

But alas!!
The weather changed, feathers got withered
Rooftop starts leaking and from the top I
stumbled

Giggles turned into silence
Surprises itself became the surprise
Pleasures were long forgotten
Treasure got stolen
Bowl crashed on the floor
And I was lost with you nowhere

Yes I was lost…baby, I got lost

Kiss on Plane

It was not any usual day
Morning breeze was cooler than usual
Roads were deserted
For a big city, it was quite unusual

The terminus was well-lit
As if welcoming me
Out of the car and I was shivering
As if put in ice

After wasting time in the waiting area
Went through all the checking formalities
And there I was entering the big tunnel
With all happiness and anxieties

Reached the plane
Searched for my seat
Felt happy
To get the window seat

Plane took off and the view was amazing
My eyes were glued to the window
But my heart was searching for someone
In the vast passengers' meadow

And it was not only my case
He was also doing the same
Suddenly the person next to me
Took my hand in his and whispered my name

It was the end of the day for me
As I got the most prayed thing on earth
My love managed to sit beside me
On the way up above the earth

The feeling was enormous
Heartbeat was pumping agile
And then came the lightest kiss on the cheek
Bursting the "happy tear" into smile

I could have asked nothing more than that
It was indeed the best journey of my life

My New Love

The lonely times we spent
The places we went

The tears we feel
The closeness which we steal

Is so dear to me
And is bringing you closer to me

You never promise for my smile
Nor will you walk for me a mile

All you give is a sweet feeling
That is so pure and thrilling

I don't fear losing you
I don't hide my tears from you

All you say is after I leave
Only happiness is left for you to have

Yes I have fallen in love again
Don't get mistaken with men
It's only the pain again